I0824251

THEN AND NOW

SCHOOL DAYS

Bobbie Kalman

LIGHTBOX
openlightbox.com

Go to **www.openlightbox.com** and enter this book's unique code.

ACCESS CODE

LBXU2499

Lightbox is an all-inclusive digital solution for the teaching and learning of curriculum topics in an original, groundbreaking way. Lightbox is based on National Curriculum Standards.

LIGHTBOX SUPPLEMENTARY RESOURCES

SHARE
Share titles within your Learning Management System (LMS) or Library Circulation System

CURRICULUM
Find national and state curriculum correlations

CITATION
Create bibliographical references following the Chicago Manual of Style

STANDARD FEATURES OF LIGHTBOX

AUDIO High-quality narration using text-to-speech system

VIDEOS Embedded high-definition video clips

ACTIVITIES Printable PDFs that can be emailed and graded

WEBLINKS Curated links to external, child-safe resources

SLIDESHOWS Pictorial overviews of key concepts

TRANSPARENCIES Step-by-step layering of maps, diagrams, charts, and timelines

INTERACTIVE MAPS Interactive maps and aerial satellite imagery

QUIZZES Ten multiple-choice questions that are automatically graded and emailed for teacher assessment

KEY WORDS Matching key concepts to their definitions

This title is part of our Lightbox digital subscription

Lightbox Grades 3–5 Subscription
ISBN 978-1-5105-5424-5

Access hundreds of Lightbox titles with our digital subscription. Sign up for a **FREE** subscription trial at **www.openlightbox.com/trial**

THEN AND NOW

SCHOOL DAYS

Contents

Old and New Schools

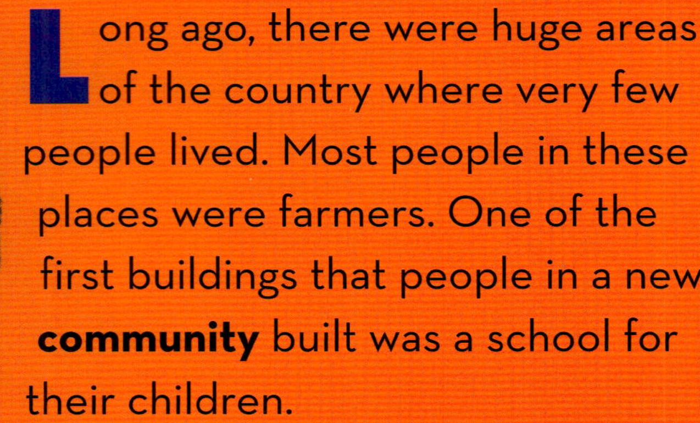

Long ago, there were huge areas of the country where very few people lived. Most people in these places were farmers. One of the first buildings that people in a new **community** built was a school for their children.

In the 1870s, about half of all U.S. teachers were women. Today, approximately 75 percent of teachers in the United States are women.

What Do You Think?

How is an old classroom the same as yours? What things do you think are different?

Long ago, some students had to wear smocks at schools, while others wore school uniforms. Smocks and uniforms are still used in some countries today.

Communities today need schools, too. These schools are different from schools long ago. For instance, new technologies are used to teach. However, in some ways, today's schools and schools from long ago are the same.

Getting to School

Students today walk, ride bicycles, or get rides to school from their parents or other adults. Many children take a school bus each day. They enjoy talking to their friends on the way to school.

A Very Long Walk!

Long ago, there were no cars, school buses, or even bicycles for getting children to school. Most children had to walk more than an hour to reach school from their home. In winter, snowstorms made it hard for them to see where they were going. Children often arrived at school feeling very cold.

Today, there are about 500,000 school buses in the United States.

How Far?

How far is your school from your home? How do you travel to school every day?

One Room or Many?

Many schoolhouses from long ago had only one room and one teacher. Electricity had not yet been invented, so a stove heated the school in winter. Open windows kept it cool on warm days.

School Rooms Today

Not many schools today have just one room. Most have several classrooms. Besides classrooms, schools also have libraries, **gymnasiums**, offices, restrooms, and lunch rooms. There are also special rooms for teachers.

In one-room schools, children of all ages learned together.

School Timeline

Schools have existed since antiquity. Over time, they changed significantly to help children around the world learn new things.

2600–2350 BC

The **Sumerians** write math books in **cuneiform**.

2070–1600 BC

In China, boys from noble families learn writing, math, music, and other disciplines in formal schools.

330–1453 AD

In the **Byzantine Empire**, teachers called *grammatistes* teach children aged 6 to 10 to read and write.

1801

The blackboard is invented.

1960

The first computer system designed to be used in schools is developed in the United States. It remains in use until 2006.

2020–2022

Children around the world are forced to switch to remote education because of the COVID-19 pandemic.

School Helpers

In a school today, there are several teachers, as well as a librarian, school nurse, principal, and caretaker. Bus drivers and crossing guards also work for schools.

Just One Teacher

In one-room schools, there was just one teacher who taught all the children. Teachers also had to keep the school clean with the help of their students. There was no principal or librarian. Parents paid the teacher's salary, and families took turns giving the teacher a place to live in their homes.

What Do They Do?

Many different people work in schools today. They all help to keep schools organized and safe.

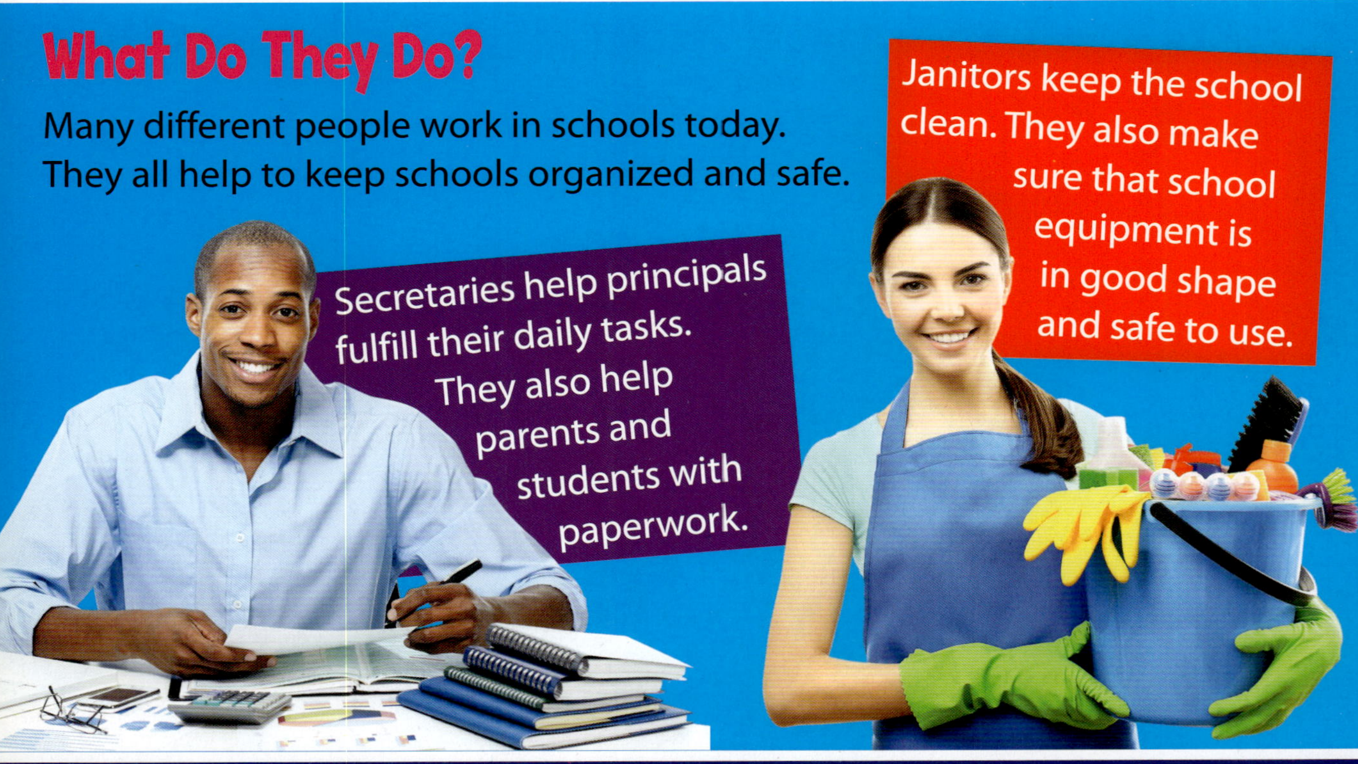

Secretaries help principals fulfill their daily tasks. They also help parents and students with paperwork.

Janitors keep the school clean. They also make sure that school equipment is in good shape and safe to use.

Sometimes, a teacher had to teach up to eight grades in one class.

Principals hire new teachers and coordinate all aspects of daily activities in a school.

School nurses take care of the physical well-being of students. They also help with health education.

A School Day

Students today come to school in the morning, have recess, and take a lunch break. Besides reading, writing, and math, they also learn science, art, social studies, music, and physical education. Children do their schoolwork with the help of books and computers.

Time to Start School!

In a one-room school long ago, the teacher rang a school bell to let the children know that school was about to begin.

Very Few Subjects

Students learned reading, writing, spelling, and arithmetic, or math, and some social studies and science. Children learned by copying what the teacher wrote on the blackboard and reciting, or repeating out loud, what they were taught. Schools had very few books because books were expensive, and farmers did not have much money. Often, each child had one book called a **primer**.

Today, some schools offer classes in advanced scientific topics such as robotics.

Average Length of School Days around the World

How many hours do you spend in school every day?

Finland	5 hours
New Zealand	6.5 hours
United States	6.8 hours
South Korea	8 hours
China	9.5 hours

Learning Tools

Many schools today have laptop computers, tablets, printers, and **interactive whiteboards** to help children read, write, spell, and learn different subjects. Students can also create reports on them.

Write and Wipe

In one-room schools, students wrote their lessons on blackboards, using chalk. After each lesson, they wiped their blackboards clean, so they could use them again. They could not keep their work and look at it again. How did this make learning harder?

Some schools use their computers during classroom teaching. Other schools allow their students to take computers home for individual work.

NEW TECHNOLOGIES IN U.S. SCHOOLS

45 PERCENT of schools have one computer for each student.

About **50 PERCENT** of schools train teachers to use new technologies.

Teachers use technology in their classrooms in more than **70 PERCENT** of schools.

About **ONE-THIRD** of school representatives think that using technology makes their students more independent.

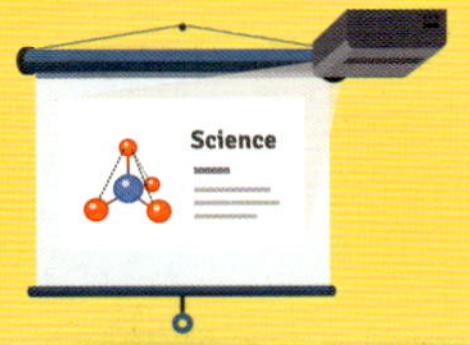

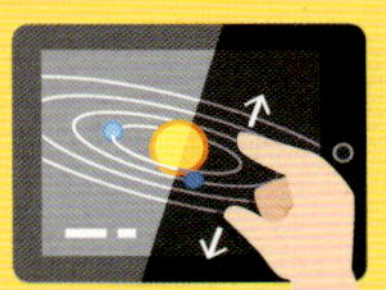

Fun Ways to Learn

Today, there are many fun ways to learn. Children draw, paint, write stories, and play musical instruments. Students from different **cultures** share their ways of life through stories, music, and art. Students also play learning games at school on computers or digital tablets.

Word Games

Spelling was an important subject long ago, just as it is today. It helped children become better readers and writers. **Spelling bees** were popular in the past and are still popular now. Children also played word games, such as **anagrams**. Anagrams helped them become better spellers.

The U.S. National Spelling Bee contest was first held in 1925.

School Systems around the World

Each country has a specific school system to ensure that children and teenagers learn everything they need to live in the modern world.

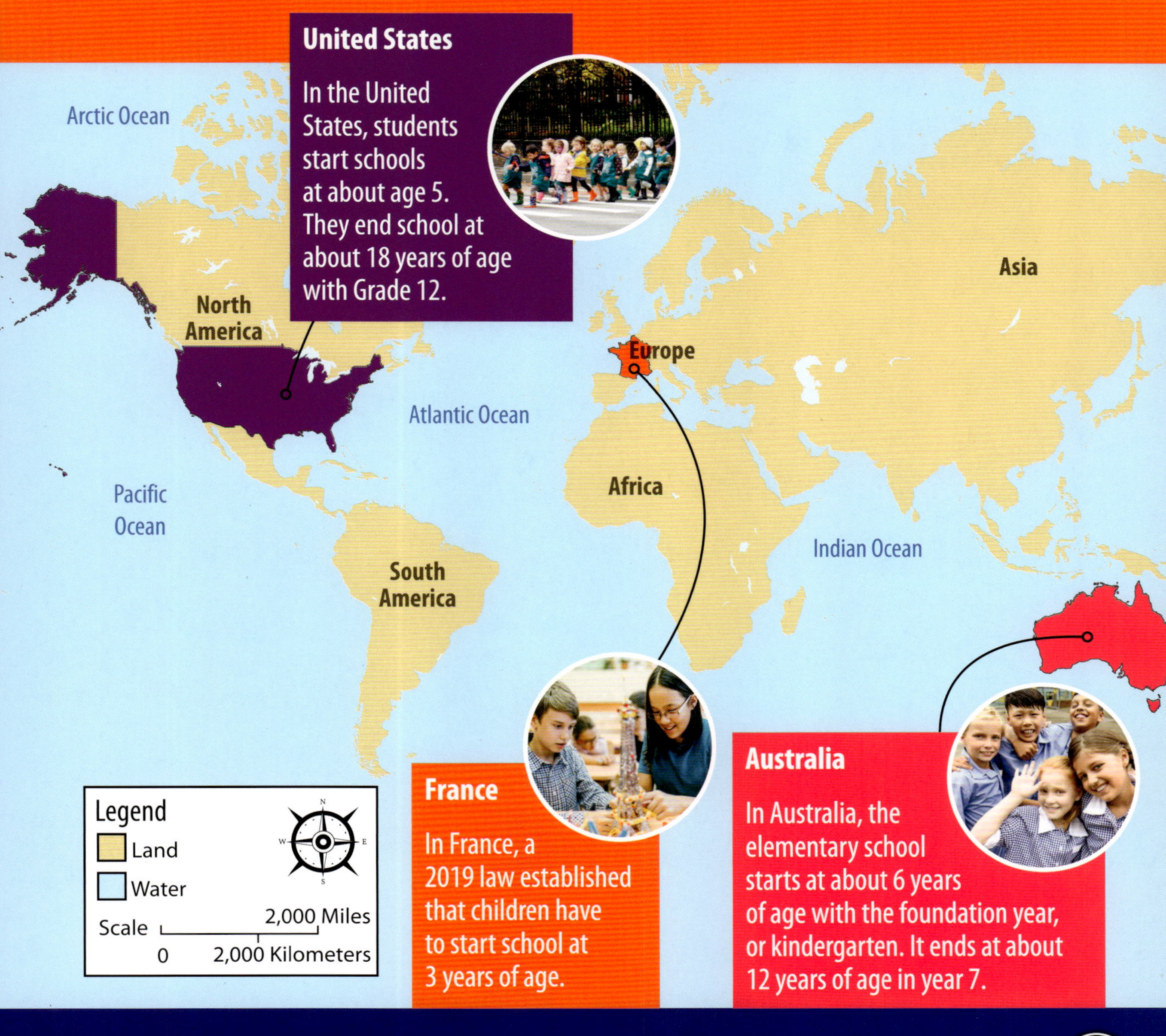

United States

In the United States, students start schools at about age 5. They end school at about 18 years of age with Grade 12.

France

In France, a 2019 law established that children have to start school at 3 years of age.

Australia

In Australia, the elementary school starts at about 6 years of age with the foundation year, or kindergarten. It ends at about 12 years of age in year 7.

Games and Sports

Games and sports are a big part of school today because exercise keeps students healthy. At recess, children play clapping and skipping games. After school, they play baseball, basketball, or soccer.

Clapping games have been played for hundreds of years.

Still Played Today

Many games and sports that were played at school in the past are still played now. Some children liked to play team sports. Others liked to play games such as hopscotch. Tag, leapfrog, and tug-of-war were other popular recess games.

How Do You Play?

What are your favorite games to play at school? Did your parents or grandparents play the same games when they were in school?

Glass marbles were often used to play different games during recess.

Hopscotch diagrams are still drawn using simple chalk.

Today, children can wear different kinds of safety equipment that children long ago did not have when playing.

In the United States, school districts decide the date for the end of the school year. This is why school ends on different days in different states.

Last Day of School

Children long ago celebrated the end of the school year. They learned special songs, put on plays, and played games with family and friends. Today, students celebrate the end of the school year in similar ways. Some have a party with their friends and look forward to coming back the following school year. Others **graduate** from elementary school and go on to middle school.

How Do You Celebrate?

Do you have a favorite way of celebrating the last day of school? What do you like to do ?

South Korea has the **longest school year** in the world. It lasts **222 days**.

In **2021**, about **3.6 million** U.S. students started **grade 5**.

Quiz

1 What do principals do?

2 When was the blackboard invented?

3 What portion of U.S. teachers were women in the 1870s?

4 What was the name of teachers in the Byzantine Empire?

5 What did France establish with a new law in 2019?

6 Who decides the date for the end of the school year in the United States?

7 How long is the average school day in China?

8 How many school buses are there in the United States today?

ANSWERS

1. They hire new teachers and coordinate all aspects of daily activities in a school.
2. In 1801 **3.** About half of all U.S. teachers **4.** Grammatistes
5. That children have to start school at 3 years of age **6.** School districts
7. 9.5 hours **8.** About 500,000

Key Words

anagrams: words or phrases created by rearranging letters of other words and phrases

Byzantine Empire: an empire that existed between 330 and 1453 AD and occupied a large area of Eastern Europe and Middle East

community: a group of people who live together in one area and share buildings, services, and a way of life

cultures: the customs, beliefs, and the way of life of a group of people

cuneiform: a system of writing composed of wedge-shaped characters used by some ancient civilizations

graduate: to finish a stage of education

gymnasiums: rooms with equipment for indoor sports or exercise

interactive whiteboards: electronic screens that can be connected to computers and projectors and are used to display images in classrooms

primer: a textbook for teaching reading or arithmetic

salary: money paid to a person on a regular basis for doing a job

spelling bees: games or competitions in which players must spell words correctly to continue

Sumerians: people who inhabited the area of ancient Mesopotamia, a region in modern-day Middle East, between 4100 and 1750 BC

Index

LIGHTBOX

SUPPLEMENTARY RESOURCES

Click on the plus icon found in the bottom left corner of each spread to open additional teacher resources.

- Download and print the book's quizzes and activities
- Access curriculum correlations
- Explore additional web applications that enhance the Lightbox experience

LIGHTBOX DIGITAL TITLES
Packed full of integrated media

VIDEOS

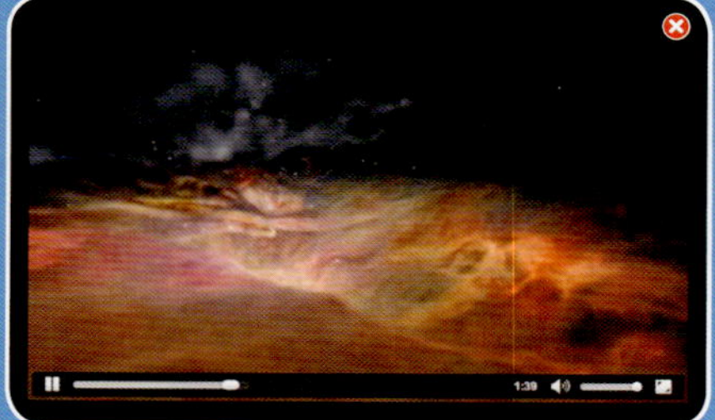

INTERACTIVE MAPS

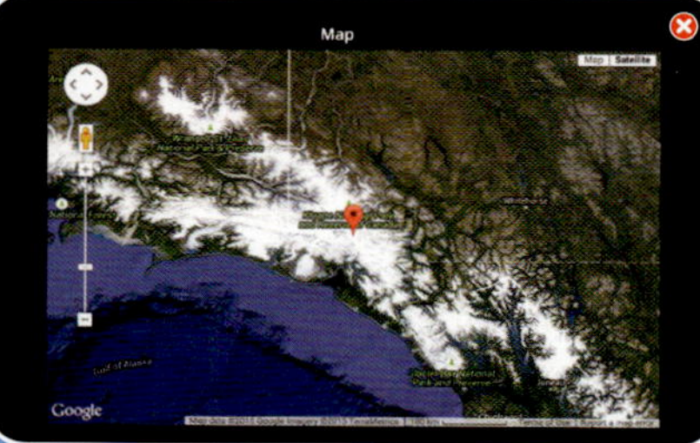

WEBLINKS

SLIDESHOWS

QUIZZES

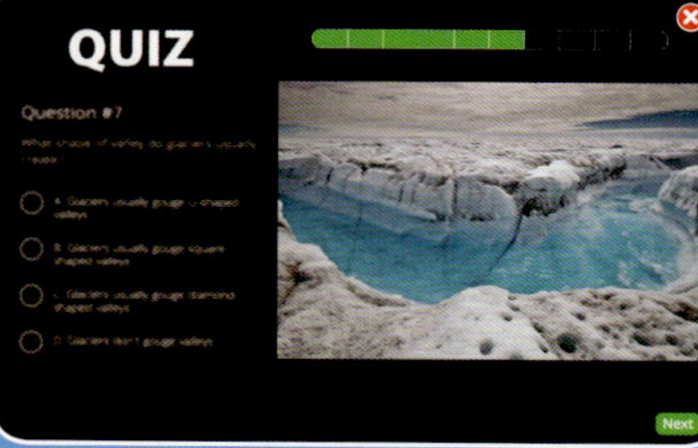

OPTIMIZED FOR

- ✓ TABLETS
- ✓ WHITEBOARDS
- ✓ COMPUTERS
- ✓ AND MUCH MORE!

Published by Lightbox Learning Inc.
276 5th Avenue, Suite 704 #917
New York, NY 10001
Website: www.openlightbox.com

Copyright ©2023 Lightbox Learning Inc.
All rights reserved. No part of this publication may be reproduced, stored in a retrieval system, or transmitted in any form or by any means, electronic, mechanical, photocopying, recording, or otherwise, without the prior written permission of the publisher.

First published by Crabtree Publishing Company in 2014

Library of Congress Control Number 2020942130

ISBN 978-1-5105-5498-6 (hardcover)
ISBN 978-1-5105-5499-3 (multi-user eBook)

Printed in Guangzhou, China
1 2 3 4 5 6 7 8 9 0 26 25 24 23 22

082022
111021

Photo Credits
Every reasonable effort has been made to trace ownership and to obtain permission to reprint copyright material. The publisher would be pleased to have any errors or omissions brought to its attention so that they may be corrected in subsequent printings. The publisher acknowledges Alamy, Getty Images, Shutterstock, Bridgeman Images, and Wikimedia Commons as its primary image suppliers for this title.

Project Coordinator Sara Cucini
Designer Ana María Vidal